IMAGES OF
HIMMLER'S NAZI CONCENTRATION CAMP GUARDS

RARE PHOTOGRAPHS FROM WARTIME ARCHIVES

Ian Baxter

Edited by Charles Markuss

Pen & Sword
MILITARY

First published in Great Britain in 2012 by
PEN & SWORD MILITARY
An imprint of
Pen & Sword Books Ltd
47 Church Street
Barnsley
South Yorkshire
S70 2AS

ISBN 978-1-84884-799-6

Typeset by Concept, Huddersfield, West Yorkshire
Printed and bound in England by CPI Group (UK) Ltd, Croydon, CR0 4YY.

Pen & Sword Books Ltd incorporates the Imprints of Pen & Sword Aviation,
Pen & Sword Family History, Pen & Sword Maritime, Pen & Sword Military, Pen & Sword Discovery,
Wharncliffe Local History, Wharncliffe True Crime, Wharncliffe Transport, Pen & Sword Select,
Pen & Sword Military Classics, Leo Cooper, The Praetorian Press, Remember When,
Seaforth Publishing and Frontline Publishing.

For a complete list of Pen & Sword titles please contact
PEN & SWORD BOOKS LIMITED
47 Church Street, Barnsley, South Yorkshire, S70 2AS, England
E-mail: enquiries@pen-and-sword.co.uk
Website: www.pen-and-sword.co.uk

Contents

About the Author

Ian Baxter is a military historian who specialises in German twentieth century military history. He has written more than twenty books including *Wolf: Hitler's Wartime Headquarters, Poland – The Eighteen Day Victory March, Panzers In North Africa, The Ardennes Offensive, The Western Campaign, The 12th SS Panzer-Division Hitlerjugend, The Waffen-SS on the Western Front, The Waffen-SS on the Eastern Front, The Red Army at Stalingrad, Elite German Forces of World War II, Armoured Warfare, German Tanks of War, Blitzkrieg, Panzer-Divisions At War, Hitler's Panzers, German Armoured Vehicles of World War Two, Last Two Years of the Waffen-SS At War, German Soldier Uniforms and Insignia, German Guns of the Third Reich, Defeat to Retreat: The Last Years of the German Army At War 1943 – 1945, Operation Bagration – the destruction of Army Group Centre, German Guns of the Third Reich, Rommel and the Afrika Korps, the Sixth Army and the Road to Stalingrad* and, most recently, *Hitler's Eastern Front Headquarters: Wolf's Lair 1941–1945.* He has written over a hundred journals including *Last days of Hitler, Wolf's Lair, Story of the V1 and V2 Rocket Programme, Secret Aircraft of World War Two, Rommel At Tobruk, Hitler's War With His Generals, Secret British Plans to Assassinate Hitler, SS at Arnhem, Hitlerjugend, Battle Of Caen 1944, Gebirgsjäger At War, Panzer Crews, Hitlerjugend Guerrillas, Last Battles in the East, Battle of Berlin,* and many more. He has also reviewed numerous military studies for publication, supplied thousands of photographs and important documents to various publishers and film production companies worldwide, and lectures to various schools, colleges and universities throughout the United Kingdom and Southern Ireland.

He currently lives in Essex with Michelle and son Felix.

Introduction

In this new addition to the popular *Images of War* series, *Himmler's Concentration Camp Guards* is a chilling portrayal of both the men and women that ran and guarded these camps. Throughout the book it unravels the decisions that led to the sophistication of a killing technique that delivered families to their deaths often by railway link just metres from the gas chambers. It will show the individual guards during their murderous activities inside these camps, and reveal another disturbing side to them relaxing in their barracks or visiting home. With the aid of many photographs and detailed captions the volume brings together a chilling often unsettling portrayal of the perpetrators of the concentration camps.

SS-Reichsführer Heinrich Himmler had embarked on something that human beings had never attempted before – the mechanised extermination of thousands of men, women and children in a matter of months. Grisly as this was, Himmler and his dominions had in fact created killing factories on an industrial scale. Yet, through these murderous activities the concentration camps actually give us a chance to understand how human beings behaved in some of the most severe conditions in history.

The book reveals that the perpetrators as a whole were not sadists lusting for power and blood nor brainwashed by propaganda, nor simply following orders. They had given themselves a personal choice to be or not to be evil. Many chose to be ruthless and brutal and actually promoted the use of violence and terror. Yet at the same time almost every male and female guard was determined from the onset to conceal as much of the gruesome knowledge as possible. In their own minds' eye it was not just their oath they were protecting, but their own credentials as human beings.

Through a series of rare photographs, captions and text, this book captures the chilling story of those that guarded the concentration camps. It brings together one of the most appalling chapters in twentieth century history, yet is a valuable addition to Holocaust studies.

Chapter 1

Recruiting and Training

Commander of the SS, *Reichsführer* Heinrich Himmler, had made considerable efforts to recruit members of the old German elite into the SS. A number of these new recruits were assigned to the new concentration camps that had sprung up across Germany. A number of new recruits joined the ranks of the black SS order and were trained at places like Dachau concentration camp. Dachau was the first regular concentration camp established by the National Socialist government and was regarded by Himmler as the first camp for political opponents who were seen as an imminent threat to the new German government. Dachau was established on 20 March 1933, and it served as a prototype and model for the other concentration camps that followed. Its basic organisation, camp layout as well as construction of buildings were developed and ordered by *SS-Brigadeführer* Theodor Eicke. In June 1933, Eicke had been made commander of Dachau concentration camp, and became a major figure in the SS. He was regarded as the architect, builder and director of the concentration camp system and ruled it with an iron fist. As a man he was stocky in appearance, blatantly brutal and ruthless, who gave off an aura of raw energy. It was here that many concentration camp guards were trained and were then assigned to other concentration camps.

Dachau was unlike any prison that the new SS recruits had been accustomed to. Unlike normal prison, the inmates did not know how long their sentence would run. In effect, they led a permanent existence of uncertainty as to when they would see freedom again. Life for the prisoners inside Dachau was brutal. The SS guards were all ordered to follow Eicke's demand for blind and absolute obedience and to treat each prisoner with fanatical hatred. By perpetually drilling his SS guards to hate the prisoners, they were able to infuse themselves with anger and recrimination and mete out severe punishments. The training these recruits were given at the camp was relentless. Not only did they learn about enemies of the state, but they were also given an in-depth indoctrination in SS philosophy and racial superiority. These ideological teachings were aimed at producing men who ardently believed in the new Aryan order. They had to listen to the commandant regularly lecturing comrades about anti-Semitism. On the bulletin boards inside the SS barracks and canteen he often saw copies of the racist newspaper, *Der Stürmer*. These propaganda newspapers had deliberately been pinned up in order to ferment hatred and violence especially against the prisoners.

All of the guards at Dachau were indoctrinated into an almost fanatical determination to serve the SS with blind allegiance. Eicke invested each guard with absolute life-and-death power over all the inmates of the camp. Rule breaking among the prisoners was classified as a crime. It was looked upon as an incitement to disobedience and each guard was given the power to hand out stringent punishments.

All SS guards were given extensive freedom to deal very harshly with any inmates they deemed to have committed a crime behind the wire. In addition to the general physical abuse meted out on the prisoners the camp commandant introduced other measures of cruelty towards these hapless individuals. Prisoners were deprived of warm food for up to four days, they were subjected to long periods of solitary confinement on a diet of bread and water. To supplement these harsh methods Eicke introduced corporal punishment into the daily routine. A prisoner would receive twenty-five strokes with the lash, carried out in the open square on specific orders from the commandant in the presence of assembled SS guards. In order to ensure every SS officer, non-commissioned officer and SS guard was instilled with the same brutal mentality as their commandant, Eicke regularly ensured that each man routinely took to punishing a prisoner with the lash without showing the slightest hesitancy, emotion and most of all, remorse. Only this way could he guarantee that the concentration camp staff would become more hardened and impersonal to the brutal code that Eicke himself had harshly implemented.

Eicke also programmed his guards to show particular hatred against Jews, immigrants, homosexuals and Jehovah Witnesses. Often, they listened whilst the commandant brazenly delivered lectures about what he considered were the most dangerous enemies of National Socialism. He instructed his guards to be brutal predominantly towards the Jews and use whatever violence necessary to keep them in check.

Although some new recruits disliked the brutality of the camp, as a whole they were inspired by its harsh order and discipline. Many were able to bury their emotions and become self-absorbed by the powers of camaraderie and loyalty to the SS. In their mind they saw the following months as a learning curve for their future. In spite of the crude and often brutal values of the SS they were given a clear example to follow. In their view they became increasingly convinced that the camp was the most effective instrument available to destroy all elements hostile to the banner of National Socialism.

The recruits also observed how Eicke had organised the inmates to work and expand the camp's economic enterprises. They saw how the commandant put to work the prisoners to construct buildings and expand the camp to include a locksmith's shop, a saddlery and a shoemaking and table shop. Eicke was a great believer that the inmates were able to endure prison with more discipline if they were allowed to work. For him working whilst enslaved was a kind of mystical declaration that self-sacrifice through endless labour brought about a kind of spiritual freedom. It was this slogan and ardent belief that prompted Eicke to display the inscription *Arbeit Macht Frei* (work makes you free) on the main entrance gate of Dachau.

For these SS guards Dachau was to mould their future in the ranks of the SS. Not only would it offer them a career, but a regular wage too. It also gave them an insight into the complete running of a concentration camp. They learned much from Eicke and the other trainers. Most importantly it strengthened their own beliefs that all the prisoners detained inside the concentration camp system were inferior and implacable enemies of the state against whom the SS were waging an unprecedented war. They had learned that the slightest vestige of sympathy towards those in the concentration camps was regarded as intolerable. They were thus compelled to conceal any type of lingering feeling or compassion against those incarcerated and follow Eicke's doctrine of being hard.

SS troops during training. Himmler had made considerable efforts to recruit members of the old German elite into the SS. A number of these new recruits were assigned to the new concentration camps that had sprung up across Germany during the 1930s. *(HITM)*

Photograph of an SS training barracks during the early part of the war. It was from here that some of the *Waffen-SS* were recruited as guards for the concentration camps. (*HITM*)

Apart from the various murderous activities of the SS inside the camps, there was also another disturbing side to them relaxing in their barracks or visiting their families and loved ones. Here an SS man poses for the camera with his daughter. *(HITM)*

An SS man poses for the camera with three female helpers at a concentration camp. The Nazis tried to maintain the illusion of female purity, depicting women as homemakers and nurturing mothers. However, with the coming of total war in 1943, the Nazis had to make changes in their policies towards women. Since German manpower was being squandered on various battlefields and slave labour also proved insufficient, the Nazis were forced to use women in a variety of different capacities, ranging from workers in the war industries to auxiliaries to the fighting troops. One such auxiliary role for women was as SS assistants in the concentration camps. *(HITM)*

SS guards during training. The SS guards were all ordered to follow Eicke's demand for blind and absolute obedience and to treat each prisoner with fanatical hatred. By perpetually drilling his SS guards to hate the prisoners, they were able to fill themselves with anger and mete out severe punishments. The training these recruits were given at the camp was relentless. Not only did they learn about enemies of the state, but also given an in-depth indoctrination in SS philosophy and racial superiority. (HITM)

An SS police unit marching, probably during a training exercise. When the Germans unleashed their attack against the Soviet Union on 22 June 1941, the Jewish problem escalated further. To deal with the Jews in Russia special SS police units were formed that consisted of Sipo-SD (Sicherheitspolizei and Sicherheitsdienst – security police and security service) personnel, Waffen-SS units, and police. Progress through the Soviet heartlands was swift and a blood bath against the Jewish population ensued.

A group of SS soldiers outside a concentration camp. By the beginning of the war concentration camps became places where millions of ordinary people were enslaved as part of the war effort. The guards were all ordered to follow blind and absolute obedience and treat each prisoner with fanatical hatred. The concentration camp commandants knew by perpetually drilling their guards to hate the prisoners, they were able to infuse themselves with anger and recrimination and mete out severe punishments. (HITM)

Three SS guards at Gross-Rosen concentration camp. These guards quickly learnt about enemies of the state, and were given an in-depth indoctrination in SS philosophy and racial superiority. *(HITM)*

SS soldiers at a field kitchen during a training exercise outside a concentration camp. The concentration camp formula for mistreating the inmates generally did not affect any of the guards psychologically. As guards they knew they were compelled to implement orders to the prisoners with horrific efficiency and not show any mercy. All guards were given extensive freedom to deal very harshly with any inmates they deemed to have committed a crime behind the wire. General physical abuse was meted out on a daily basis, amid other measures of cruelty upon these hapless individuals. (*HITM*)

Slovakian guards at a guard post leading into a concentration camp. Many foreign guards were recruited into the concentration camp system in order to supplement the shortage of manpower during the German war effort. *(USHMM)*

SS guards at a barracks. Many of the recruits that had arrived at these camps had opted to work in the concentration camp system, not because they were trying to avoid military service, but simply because they were accustomed to the tasks, however brutal or psychologically disturbing they were. These men looked upon their duty merely as a job and performed all their tasks hiding behind the facade 'that they were only following orders'. (HITM)

An interesting photograph showing the Inspector of Concentration Camps *SS-Brigadefuhrer* Richard Gluecks holding a briefcase with other SS officers. Gluecks was a ruthless and fanatic SS officer who believed wholeheartedly in the Nazi vision. From his office he planned and gossiped with his associates about the future SS and was ever eager to help expand the concentration camp system. (*USHMM*)

A view of the perimeter of Dachau concentration camp showing the barbed wire entanglements that ominously surrounded the camp. Dachau was the first regular concentration camp established by the National Socialist government and was regarded by Himmler as the first camp for political opponents who were seen as an imminent threat to the new German government. Dachau was established on 20 March 1933, and it served as a prototype and model for the other concentration camps that followed. Its basic organisation, camp layout and construction of buildings was developed and ordered by *SS-Brigadeführer* Theodor Eicke. In June 1933, Eicke had been made commander of Dachau concentration camp, and became a major figure in the SS.

Chapter Two

Early Concentration Camps

In order to retain political prisoners and other elements regarded by the Reich as hostile to the new Nazi regime, Hitler had decided that concentration camps would be erected throughout Germany. The first concentration camp built for this purpose was Dachau, which was established on 20 March 1933 and served as a prototype and model for the other concentration camps that followed. Dachau was capable of accommodating up to 5,000 persons. Anyone considered 'undesirable' to the Nazi cause, such as all the Communists, *Reichsbanner* ('State Banner', an ineffective republican organisation supported mainly by the Social Democratic Party until disbanded and suppressed in March 1933) and Social Democratic functionaries, were to be contained there.

Over the next few months and years that followed a number of concentration camps were erected all over Germany. There were camps such as at Sachsenhausen built in 1936, Buchenwald in 1937, Flossenburg, Mauthausen, Neuengamme in 1938, and Ravensbruck, Stutthof and Westerbork completed in 1939. There were so many people sent to theses new concentration camps that almost every community in Germany had members taken there.

After September 1939, with the beginning of the Second World War, concentration camps became places where millions of ordinary people were enslaved as part of the war effort. The guards were all ordered to follow blind and absolute obedience and treat each prisoner with fanatical hatred. The concentration camp commandants knew by perpetually drilling their guards to hate the prisoners, they were able to infuse themselves with anger and recrimination and mete out severe punishments. For these new guards entering the realms of the concentration camp system for the first time it was a way of testing their morals and inner self belief to do their duty. They had learnt about enemies of the state, and been given an in-depth indoctrination in SS philosophy and racial superiority. The concentration camp formula for mistreating the inmates generally did not affect any of the guards psychologically. As guards they knew they were compelled to implement orders to the prisoners with horrific efficiency and not show any mercy. All guards were given extensive freedom to deal very harshly with any inmates they deemed to have committed a crime behind the wire. General physical abuse was meted out on a daily occurrence, and other measures of cruelty upon these hapless individuals were also handed out. Prisoners were deprived of warm food for up to four days, they were subjected to long periods of solitary confinement on a diet of bread and water. To supplement these harsh methods the commandant of the camp introduced corporal punishment into the daily routine. A prisoner would receive twenty-five strokes with the lash, carried out in the open on specific orders of the commandant in the presence of assembled guards. In order to ensure every officer, non-commissioned officer and guard was instilled with the same brutal mentality as their commandant, each man routinely took to punishing a prisoner with the lash without showing the slightest hesitancy, emotion and, most of all, remorse. Only this way would it guarantee that the concentration camp staff would become more hardened and impersonal to the brutal code of the SS.

Many of the guards that arrived at these camps had opted to work in the concentration camp system, not because they were trying to avoid military service, but simply because they were accustomed to the tasks, however brutal or psychologically disturbing they were. These men looked upon their duty merely as a job and performed all their tasks hiding behind the facade 'that they were only following orders'. In this way they were able to exhibit cruelty towards their victims and think that they would somehow not be accountable for their actions. By blaming the system they subconsciously believed they could undertake almost any crime they saw fit and rid their moral conscience of any wrongdoing.

The majority of the personnel that joined this brutal system were young men aged between twenty-six and forty, mostly married with small children. Many of these young men could at any time have chosen to leave and be posted into the armed services, but they stayed, not realising for one moment the phychological impact these camps would have, leading to mass shootings, mass burials, gassing victims in makeshift buildings or in adapted experimental road vehicles, the development of massive factory-like killing centres and the disposal of the dead in specially-built crematoria. Almost every man that came to the concentration camp was determined from the outset to conceal as much of the hidden atrocities as long as possible to the outside world. In their own minds it was not just their oath they were protecting, but their own credentials as human beings. In order to make it easier for them and lessen the psychological impact, they tried not to connect their families or loved ones to some of the gruesome tasks that lay ahead, but in the main wanted to get the job done and go home.

For many of the guards in the concentration camp system during the early years of the Reich it was a foundation for greater and more barbaric measures to come. They themselves would evolve in a system that would not only incarcerate and work their inmates to death, but would eventually be ordered to mass execute by shooting to digging large mass graves to gassing in makeshift buildings to eventually erecting massive factory-like killing centres to gas thousands of people in specially built crematories.

(Opposite) SS-Reichsführer Heinrich Himmler with his SS troops. Himmler was commander-in-chief of the SS and became the architect of genocide. (USHMM)

SS-Reichsführer Heinrich Himmler with his SS troops. During the late 1930s Himmler went to great lengths to expand the SS and concentration camp system. Literally thousands of men were recruited as concentration camp guards in order to contain those considered hostile to the Nazi regime. *(USHMM)*

SS guards relax in the sun, probably after a hard day's killing. After September 1939, with the beginning of the Second World War, concentration camps became places where millions of ordinary people were enslaved as part of the war effort. *(HITM)*

A view of a wooden building and surrounding garden. This was more than likely the home of the commandant of the Hinzert concentration camp. Many SS officers tried their utmost to make their living quarters as homely as possible. This was not only a way of averting their gaze from the daily horrors in the camps, but was also an attempt to bring about a kind of normality in an abnormal surrounding. (*USHMM*)

A group of SS officers, a dog and a woman pose for the camera at the Gross-Rosen concentration camp. In the main the SS were not assigned their tasks because of any type of exceptional qualities they held. The anti-Semitism they held within was part of their culture and had been nurtured over years of intense propaganda, and these people were certainly not brainwashed. Most were married, and the majority did not have a criminal record. They had simply volunteered to serve in the SS in a camp where they were ordered to carry out their duties loyally and unquestioningly. *(USHMM)*

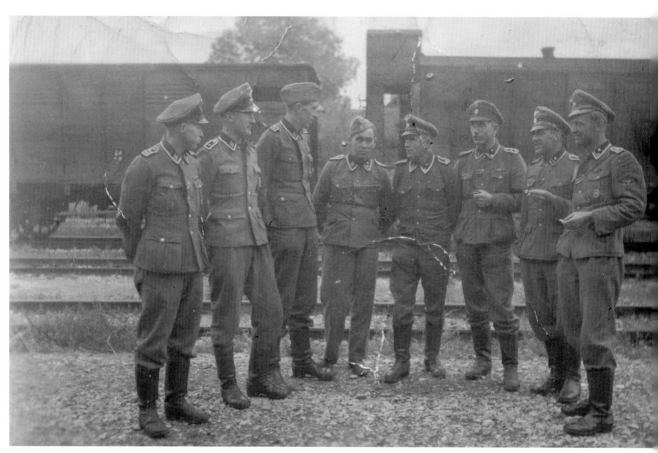

SS troops at a railway terminal prior to the transportation of human cargo to one of the many concentration camps that littered Germany and Eastern Europe. Note the empty railway cars behind them. (*HITM*)

SS officers during a ceremony in 1941. (*HITM*)

Buchenwald gallows being erected. Quite typically these SS men looked upon their duty merely as a job and performed all their tasks hiding behind the facade 'that they were only following orders'. In this way they were able to behave barbarically but still think that they would somehow not be accountable for their actions. By blaming the system they subconsciously believed they could undertake almost any crime they saw fit and rid their moral conscience of any wrongdoing. (*USHMM*)

A group photograph showing some of the SS personnel that ran Buchenwald concentration camp. Working at a concentration camp like Buchenwald many of the SS never presented themselves as mindless automatons that just followed orders. Although they were massively influenced by the propaganda of the times, it is quite evident from extensive research that they made a series of personal choices. They carried on working at camps like these not just because they were ordered to, but because posted to a concentration camp meant it would avoid any risk to life, such as fighting on a battlefield. There is no record of any member of the SS refusing or resisting on moral grounds to work in the camps. They could have easily rejected a concentration camp posting and been ordered to the front, but the majority were content living a life in the camp, killing and torturing those they regarded had no intrinsic claim to life. (*USHMM*)

Members of the SS and police speak among themselves during a roll call at Buchenwald concentration camp. (*USHMM*)

Newly arrived prisoners at the Buchenwald concentration camp. SS guards can be seen conferring with police personnel while the prisoners wait before being assigned to their barracks. (*USHMM*)

A close-up portrait of three SS officers at a barracks at the Gross-Rosen concentration camp. (*USHMM*)

An SS officer walking through the vicinity of a concentration camp. (*HITM*)

Two photographs showing Commandant Hermann Pister, one showing him accompanied by three SS officers possibly outside an administration office and the other at a bunker at the Hinzert concentration camp. (*USHMM*)

Four SS officers pose for the camera standing outside a barracks at the Gross-Rosen concentration camp. (*USHMM*)

A group portrait of ethnic German guards at the Belzec concentration camp. (*USHMM*)

A group portrait of SS personnel in front of barracks at the Hinzert concentration camp. (*USHMM*)

Newly arrived Polish prisoners are seen undressing whilst SS guards supervise. Although the guards rarely saw the prisoners as individuals, they often avoided at any price talking to those who were about to die. (*USHMM*)

SS guards stand in formation outside the commandant's house near the Belzec concentration camp. (*USHMM*)

SS man Papka at Gross-Rosen concentration camp poses for the camera with puppies. In spite of the ruthless manner in which these SS men behaved in the concentration camps many of the SS were actually inspired by the thought of home, believing that when they got leave they would be able to recapture the life they had enjoyed before their posting to the camps. But it was not possible. The concentration camp system had altered them. Though they never sought to change their comfortable existence in the camp, it was quite apparent of the psychological burden they had to carry. They deliberately manipulated and repressed their moral scruples. The majority felt bound by honour and duty to the SS order, and were compelled to carry out their gruesome crimes in secret. The psychological impact on some of them was often severe, because they were exposed on a daily basis to the horrors. (USHMM)

Chapter Three

Reinhard Camps

When the Germans unleashed their attack against the Soviet Union on 22 June 1941, the Jewish problem escalated further. For the Nazi empire the prospect of a war against Russia entailed a transition from one policy of murder to another. This in effect brought about the most radical ideas imaginable in the eyes of the SS. As Hitler had explained to his generals just a few months prior to the invasion, the war would be no normal war; it was an ideological war of extermination. In the eyes of Hitler the Soviet Union represented the home of Bolshevism and international Jewry, which needed to be both rooted out and destroyed. To deal with the Jews in Russia four *Einsatzgruppen* (action groups) were formed that consisted of *Sipo-SD* personnel, *Waffen-SS* units and police. Progress through the Soviet heartlands was swift and a blood bath against the Jewish population ensued. Although the killings of the Jews by shooting proved highly effective in terms of the large numbers murdered, commanders in the field soon became aware it had many disadvantages as a method of mass murder. Firstly, the killings were difficult to conceal and were often witnessed by large numbers of unauthorised persons, including the *Wehrmacht*, who often complained bitterly at the brutality. This was not so much out of sympathy for those being executed but for the psychological effects it had on the men. The stress it caused among many of the participants was so widespread that it often resulted in a number of soldiers consuming large amounts of alcohol whilst they killed. Others, however, had nervous breakdowns, and there were incidents of numerous suicides. Some men simply could not face the strain and refused to take part in the slaughter. These men were regarded as weak and were quickly weeded out by their commanding officers and posted elsewhere on the front. They might have been deemed by their superiors as cowards, but no one was punished for such refusal. With every soldier that refused to take part in the killings, there was always another to replace him. Virtually all men accepted their orders automatically, and soon became accustomed to the daily butchery of killing men, women and children. Some were actually addicted to the killings, whilst the majority accepted it as a sacred order, and 'just got on with it'.

At higher levels, however, there were occasional objections, especially from the *Wehrmacht*, but these complaints were generally political or tactical. Himmler made it clear to the *Wehrmacht* that they would have to simply accept the wholesale liquidations in the East as policy. It was a matter of ideology versus military or economic needs and for this reason they would have to accept the fact and co-operate.

Whilst the *Wehrmacht* accepted the killings in the East, the SS were aware that they needed a better technique for murdering in large numbers very quickly, and as anonymously as possible. They needed something cheaper, tidier and quicker, which would also be less distressing to the executioners. Even the *Reichsführer* was all too well aware of the problems of mass execution. In fact, in August 1941, whilst near Minsk he witnessed a mass killing and nearly fainted during the spectacle. He commented to a commander in the field that the execution was inhumane and effects on the troops would lower morale. He made it clear he wanted a more effective method of killing such, as explosives or gas.

The use of gas was not a new method used by the Nazi state. In fact, a special department known as T4, which had organised the 'Euthanasia Programme', first used gassing installations in Germany to kill the insane and incurably ill. The programme was a complete success and ran for two years, but due to growing public opinion against euthanasia in Germany the killings were reluctantly suspended. Now it was proposed that this method of killing should be used outside Germany against enemies of the state, especially those from the East. The invasion of the Soviet Union in the summer of 1941 gave access to thousands of Jews and other creeds regarded by the Nazis as 'subhuman', and plans were immediately utilised to kill as many as possible using the method of gas.

Over the coming weeks, whilst the *Wehrmacht* continued to advance ever deeper into Russia, gas was used for the first time by the *Einsatzgruppen*. A special vehicle had been built to resemble an ambulance or refrigerator truck that was airtight. The victims would be placed in the cabin and carbon monoxide was introduced by means of a pipe. By the autumn of 1941, the first gas van prepared for the Eastern Front was first tested on Russian prisoners of war in Sachsenhausen concentration camp. This crude method of systematic annihilation of human beings was considered the best and most effective means of mass killing whilst its troops pushed forward through the Soviet Union. It was also deemed to help the special commando killing squads achieve large scale murders without ever needing to look into the eyes of their victims as they gunned them down. Although many thousands of Jews and Russians were captured and herded into the new gas vans and murdered, they were not very popular with the SS since they were deemed more unpleasant to operate than mass executions by shooting. However, they were to remain the preferred method of liquidating the Jews in Russia and intended to lighten the task of carrying out the killing operations in the occupied territories.

Gas vans were also used in the first extermination centre, which was built in the nearby village of Chelmno. The first transport of Jews arrived in lorries on

5 December 1941. Over a five month period some 55,000 Jews from the nearby Lodz ghetto were gassed along with at least 5,000 gypsies.

Whist the Chelmno extermination centre had been geared to the liquidation of Jews in the surrounding district in the Warthegau, the vast majority of Polish Jews, including many deported or escaped from the Warthegau, were in the General Government. A total of some 2.3 million of them were now contained in ghettos there.

At the Wannsee conference held in Berlin in January 1942, it was agreed that it would be the Jews in the General Government (occupied Poland) that would be dealt with first. This large unincorporated area was deemed the dumping ground for all undesirables and enemies of the state. It was here that the first deportations of Poles and Jews were sent in their thousands. In fact, preparations had already been undertaken and the Nazi leadership was under no illusion that it required great organisational skills to implement the effective means of mass murder. Already a pool of experts had been drafted in to undertake this mammoth task.

From the onset they were aware that the problems of transporting large numbers of Jews to Russia, and liquidating them would be a logistical nightmare, especially when the war in Russia had not been won. They soon came to the conclusion that it was more practical to transport German and other Jews to Poland and to kill them immediately, rather than send them further East. It was therefore suggested that a series of extermination camps, not unlike that of Auschwitz, was to be constructed in Poland, to where those that were deemed unfit for work would be transported and killed.

The preparation for the extermination of Jews in Poland had been planned at the Wannsee Conference. It was here in Berlin where a special organisation, later named 'Operation Reinhard', was established in Lublin. Operation Reinhard was the code name given for the systemic annihilation of Polish Jews in the General Government, and it would mark the beginning of the most deadly phase of the programme, the use of extermination camps. The SS and police leader of the district of Lublin, *SS-Oberstgruppenführer* Odilo Globocnik, was appointed the commander of the operation. Globocnik was a ruthless and fanatic SS officer who believed whole-heartedly in the Nazi vision. From his office he planned and gossiped with his associates about the future SS colonisation of the East and the task of preparing the extermination of the Jews in the General Government.

In order to undertake such an action against the Jews, killing centres were to be utilised for Operation Reinhard. Globocnik set to work immediately and brought in people who had been assigned to the euthanasia program that had the knowledge and experience in setting up and operating factories for mass murder. Planning and construction of three death camps were put forward, which included sites at Belzec,

Sobibor and Treblinka. All three camps were to be unique, as their purpose was different from other concentration camps.

The first of the Operation Reinhard extermination camps in Poland was located in the south-east of the district of Lublin called Belzec. The entire camp was to be guarded by around eighty guards, all of whom were Ukrainian. Famed for their brutality, many of these Ukrainians having previously fought in the Red Army, were now to be trained by the Germans, and allowed this opportunity to escape the terrible conditions of the POW camps. They were all trained at Trawniki, a special camp near Lublin specifically set-up to prepare and train Ukrainians and ethnic Germans for their role in the *Reinhard Aktion*. These volunteers were nicknamed by the local population 'Trawniki men' or 'Askaries'. The Germans called them *Hilfswillige* (literally, willing helper), or 'Hiwis' for short.

Some of the Ukrainian guards were organised into two battalions with four companies each, about 1,000 men altogether. The size of the company was roughly 100–200 men. One or two of the companies were stationed mainly in Lublin for security duties, whilst the others were sent mainly to guard labour camps in the Lublin district. Their duties comprised supporting the local police units, carrying out deportations, and mass executions of Jews. Their first assignment to the Reinhard camps were at Belzec where a company-sized unit of around 100 men was allocated to the camp.

The camp commandant, Christian Wirth, had arrived at Belzec before Christmas 1941, bringing with him a group of about ten euthanasia specialists, including the notorious chemist, Dr Kallmeyer. Within months of his arrival Wirth was adapting previous killing techniques with the use of gas. By February 1942 two gassing tests were undertaken at Belzec, the first with Zyklon B (hydrogen cyanide gas) and the second with bottled carbon monoxide.

Wirth realised that by killing large numbers of people in one physical place he had broken completely from the conventional design of a concentration camp. Because the vast majority of arrivals would be alive only for a matter of a few hours a large complex of wooden and concrete buildings, such as those found at Auschwitz, would no longer be required. A death camp, unlike a concentration camp, needed only a few facilities to operate effectively. After all, its sole purpose was the wholesale liquidation of many people at any one time, and this would require only a small space.

Wirth was aware that the smooth functioning of a death camp required something more than a concentration camp. Whereas most prisoners that were sent to places like Auschwitz and Dachau knew that they were being incarcerated, at a death camp Wirth wanted to conceal the true purpose of the place from the new arrivals for as long as possible. So within the camp he had the gas chamber building camouflaged and hidden behind trees and a wire fence.

He knew that by building a large gas chamber the killing process would not only spare his own men from psychological suffering, but more importantly mean fewer personnel would be required to actually run the camp. He would employ a number of healthy Jewish slave labourers selected upon arrival to the camp and put them to work burying bodies, sorting the vast quantities of clothing and valuables, and cleaning the gas chambers.

The Belzec death camp finally began its operations on 17 March 1942 with a transport of some fifty goods wagons containing Jews from Lublin. Between March and the end of April, thousands of Jews from the Lublin and Lemberg districts were successfully exterminated in Belzec. It was a factory on an industrial scale, and Wirth looked upon the operation as a director of a plant where the raw goods were delivered, processed and then stored. Wirth had realised his *Reichsführer*'s dream that the desired end result would finally see the complete annihilation of the Jewish race. Yet, even to someone as shrewd and evil like Wirth, he knew that Belzec alone would not be sufficient to deal with the numbers of people scheduled to be sent there.

So, in March whilst the first trainloads of Jews were being readied for Belzec, another Reinhard death camp was being constructed. It was near the small village of Sobibor in a wooded area on the Chelmno-Wlodawa railway line a few miles south of Wlodawa. The installation was an enlarged and improved version of Belzec with the same general layout. *SS-Hauptsturmführer* Franz Stangl, a thirty-four-year-old Austrian graduate of the Hartheim euthanasia centre, was appointed as commandant.

By the summer of 1942, both Sobibor and Belzec were running simultaneously, and despite the technical problems of machinery breaking down and the problems with body disposal, the Reinhard camps were achieving what they had been intended for, the wholesale mass extermination of Jews.

Whilst Sobibor and Belzec continued to operate at full capacity, a far bigger installation was being prepared for construction that would be intended to receive all transports from Warsaw and Bialystok ghettos. The site chosen was near the small village of Treblinka in the north-eastern part of the General Government. The plan of the camp was almost identical to Sobibor, but with some improvements.

As with all concentration camps erected throughout the *Reich* and Poland they were run cruelly, and Treblinka would be no exception. The guards were all ordered to follow blind and absolute obedience and treat each prisoner with fanatical hatred. Many of the new recruits that were picked for Treblinka and indeed for all the *Aktion Reinhard* camps were individually selected on the basis of their previous experience in the euthanasia programme. The main personnel had been administered directly by the officers of T4, all of whom boasted an exceptional record. In total, only ninety-six SS out of 400 had been chosen to run the three camps.

For these new SS recruits entering the realms of the concentration camp system for the first time it was a way of testing their morals and inner self belief to do their duty. They had learnt about enemies of the state, and been given an in-depth indoctrination in SS philosophy and racial superiority. These ideological teachings were aimed at producing men who ardently believed in the new Aryan order.

Many of the personnel that came to Treblinka had already served in other camps like Belzec and Sobibor, and had a deep insight into the complete running of a concentration camp. The more ambitious concentration camp guards learned much from their commandants and were determined, if they were to progress further through the ranks, to strengthen their own beliefs that all the prisoners detained inside the concentration camp system were inferior and implacable enemies of the state against whom the SS were waging an unprecedented war. They were totally aware that the slightest vestige of sympathy towards those in the concentration camps was regarded by the SS as intolerable. They were thus compelled to conceal any type of lingering feeling or compassion against those incarcerated and follow the doctrine of being hard. For a number of SS guards it was not just a personal crusade to rid the world of the enemies of the state, but it was more an ardent desire to be part of a membership of a privileged order like the SS that was fixated on command and obedience. In the realms of the SS they were resolute in carrying out, with maximum efficiency, any orders it laid down, no matter how brutal they were against mankind.

For these men, undertaking such acts of brutality, there were special inducements such as extra rations of cigarettes, schnapps and sausage. Some, however, needed no urging to bloody their hands, and went about killing and abusing their victims at will. Here they were about to embark on the mechanised extermination of literally hundreds of thousands of men, women and children in only a matter of months. As in any industrial operation, their superiors were well aware that such widespread murder could only achieve the desired end result if the trains sent people on schedule, if the gas chambers worked completely in synchronisation with each other, and could cope with the vast volumes of new arrivals. Already chaos had ensued at Belzec because it did not have sufficient gas chambers to deal with the huge numbers of people arriving there daily. The problem had become so bad that in June 1942 the camp shut down for a month and new gas chambers were hastily built. At Sobibor, the problem was both the size of the gas chambers and transportation by rail to the camp. Much now depended on Treblinka to ease the burden placed on the Reinhard camps.

The clearing of the Warsaw ghetto and the organising of the transportation of the Jews to the death camps within Poland was an immense undertaking. For Doctor I. Eberl, the camp Commandant at Treblinka, and his subordinates the easiest and most practical means was to dupe the Jews and murder them as quickly as possible.

Each member of the camp was trained to dupe all new arrivals into believing they had alighted at a disinfecting stop where they would be treated as a precaution against disease, and were then to be hurried through the camp to their deaths as quickly as possible.

Within a year, some 800,000 people had been sent directly to their death in the gas chambers. Though the figures are comparatively much lower than Wirth would ever have wanted, it was no less an inexcusable number of people killed. It had become the second largest killing centre in the Nazi regime, and would have far exceeded that of Auschwitz had it remained fully operational through 1944. But its mission was complete and its achievements in the eyes of the SS were an astounding success. They had not only cleansed the General Government in just over one year but incredibly kept the erection of the camp and the activities there secret from the overwhelming majority of victims. As for the guards, when the camp was finally shut down at the end of 1943, the majority had seen the liquidation of hundreds of thousands of Jews as a just cause. They were able to praise their efforts because they had convinced themselves that the Jew was a racial-biological threat and a political enemy.

SS guards in the snow during the early part of the war on a training exercise. (*HITM*)

Out on the Eastern Front and SS forces prepare to undertake an action. When the Germans unleashed their attack against the Soviet Union on 22 June 1941, the Jewish problem escalated further. For the Nazi empire the prospect of a war against Russia entailed a transition from one policy of murder to another. (*HITM Archive*)

SS-Polizei forces preparing to undertake an action in Russia. In the eyes of Hitler the Soviet Union represented the home of Bolshevism and international Jewry, which he said needed to be both rooted out and destroyed. (*HITM Archive*)

SS-Polizeitruppen during operations in the East. Here the troops are scouring the countryside for partisans and other elements regarded by the SS as hostile to the Nazi State. *(HITM Archive)*

SS forces in a wooded area. Virtually all the SS accepted their orders automatically, and soon became accustomed to the daily butchery of killing men, women and children. Some were actually addicted to the killings, whilst the majority accepted it as a sacred order, and 'just got on with it'. *(HITM Archive)*

Barry, the St Bernard dog, sitting for a photograph, probably taken by *SS-Oberscharführer* Kurt Franz. Barry had been trained by Franz to be particularly ferocious, and upon his command he would attack Jews, biting at their bodies and sinking its sharp teeth in the victim's genitals, occasionally ripping them off. *(HEART)*

Another photograph of Barry, this time as a pup. Often Franz would be seen roaming Treblinka with Barry, some-times strolling along the platform with a double-barrelled shotgun in his hand and Barry following behind. *(HEART)*

Because of the huge flood of transports more prisoners were required to be selected for work detail to bury the thousands of people that were gassed and shot. *Kommandant* Eberl ordered that more burial pits were required to be dug, and this was only partially solved by an excavator, seen here in this photograph moving sand and earth in the pits. *(ARC)*

Two photographs taken of the Treblinka excavator. The excavator had been brought over from Treblinka I and was used every day to help bury the dead and dig corpse pits. The excavator was built by Menck & Hambrocka type 'Ma', produced between 1933 and 1944. These photos were taken by Stangl's deputy Kurt Franz. The photos were found in his Treblinka album 'Schöne Zeiten' (Pleasant Times). (ARC)

Two photographs showing SS men on the buckets of the excavator. These photographs were probably taken in the first half of 1943. At least two types of excavators were used in Treblinka, bucket and cable excavators. It was later realised that the bucket excavator was not very effective for digging burial pits. *(ARC)*

Deportation of Jews from the General Government either in the late winter of 1942, or early 1943. (*HITM Archive*)

Two photographs showing Jewish men, women and children with their belongings preparing to board a train to an unknown destination. During mid-1942 a whole series of resettlement 'actions' were being conducted right across occupied Poland. These actions saw the vast majority of Jews now being sent directly to Belzec, Sobibor and Treblinka. Around ninety-five per cent of all arrivals at these camps were dead within three hours. *(HITM Archive)*

Two photographs showing two SS officers belonging to an unidentified police unit in the East during the winter of 1942. Throughout 1942 and the following year the SS police and special action killing squads undertook various operations combing the countryside for Jews and partisans and any other people they regarded that were hostile elements to their regime. *(HITM Archive)*

(*Below*) A photograph, taken probably during the late summer of 1942, showing Stangl and his deputy Franz at a doorway to the SS barracks. Stangl is wearing his familiar white tunic and holding an oxide whip. (*ARC*)

A posed photograph of Eberl, the first commandant of Treblinka, who ruled the camp with an iron fist. As soon as he took command he was determined to deliver an exceptional killing rate that far outweighed that of any other camp in the Nazi empire. (*HEART*)

A portrait photograph of Hermann Felfe. He oversaw the construction of the first water tower in Camp I. of Treblinka. *(HEART)*

A portrait photograph of Alfred Forker. He was posted to Treblinka in 1942 and undertook guard duties in Camp II. His duties also included the sorting yard. (*HEART*)

SS-Unterscharführer Fritz Schmidt disembarking from a vehicle in the grounds of Treblinka. Schmidt operated the gas chamber engines in the camp. (*HEART*)

SS-Oberscharführer Willy Matzig. He was book-keeper/accountant and was one of Stangl's two senior administrative assistants. His office was in Stangl's quarters. He was also part of the squad that received prisoners on the platform (known as the 'ramp') when deportations arrived. (*HEART*)

SS-Rottenwachmeister Willy Grossmann. His main duties were in Camp II of Treblinka and he also received prisoners on the platform when deportations arrived. (*HEART*)

SS-Sturmbannführer Christian Wirth (middle) accompanied by other SS officers during a tour of one of the Reinhard camps. Wirth soon earned himself a reputation and was nicknamed 'savage Christian'. Wirth realised that by killing large numbers of people in one physical place he had broken completely from the conventional design of a concentration camp. *(HEART)*

Two photographs, one showing the fake Treblinka station and the other showing SS and Ukrainian guards posing for the camera outside the station in the early spring of 1943. At Christmas Stangl had ordered the construction of a fake railway station. The commandant wanted to enhance the illusion and deception in order to fool the new arrivals into believing they had arrived at a genuine station to a transit camp. A clock painted with numerals and a hand that never moved, a ticket-window was constructed, various timetables and arrows indicating train connections to Warsaw, Wolwonoce, and to Bialystock were plastered on the walls of the sorting barracks. There were fake doors and windows installed, a Waiting Room, Information Telegraph Office, Station Manager, Rest Rooms, and there were many trees and flowerbeds. (HEART)

This photo was taken in August 1942 when Pötzinger visited the Treblinka cook August Hengst and his wife Augusta in Warsaw. During an interrogation after the war Hengst spoke about this visit. He was allowed to wear civilian clothes, and he had an apartment in Warsaw where he often welcomed visitors from Treblinka. At this time Hengst was busy getting food and other goods for the Treblinka camp staff. From time to time he had to travel to Treblinka. One day camp commander Stangl forbade the wearing of civilian clothes. However, when Pötzinger and Pinnemann were visiting, they decided to go to a photographic studio in the same road, where this photo was taken. *(ARC)*

The camp zoo constructed near the Ukrainian barracks on the orders of Stangl in the early summer of 1943. Here the SS spent their leisure time sitting on wooden benches and tables relaxing and enjoying looking at the animals. *(ARC)*

A posed photograph of, from left to right, *SS-Unterscharführer* Paul Bredow (Head of 'Barracks A', which was the clothing sorting barracks), *SS-Unterscharführer* Willi Mentz (Assigned to Camp II in the summer of 1942 and then to Camp I as chief *Landwirtschaftskommando* (Agricultural Command)), *SS-Unterscharführer* Max Moller (Posted to Camp I as ordinance, 'Undressing Yard', and farming), and *SS-Scharführer* Josef Hirtreiter, nicknamed 'Sepp' by his comrades (he was appointed to Treblinka in October 1942 until October 1943, his main duties were in Camp II). (*HEART*)

SS guards pose for the camera during Christmas festivities. (*HITM*)

At a concentration camp and SS field kitchen can be seen. (*HITM*)

This ammunition storeroom in Treblinka was located between the two SS barracks. It was built during the first phase of the camp as a concrete cube. In spring 1943 a second storey was added, containing a water tank to supply new showers for the SS staff. During the revolt the SS barracks burned down. This photo was taken by Kurt Franz, after the revolt. (ARC)

Three guards stand in front of the main building at Sobibor. Sobibor was constructed in a wooded area on the Chelmno-Wlodawa railway line a few miles south of Wlodawa. The installation was an enlarged and improved version of Belzec with the same general layout. Sobibor officially became operational in mid-May 1942. By the summer of 1942, both Sobibor and Belzec were running simultaneously, and despite the technical problems of machinery breaking down and the problems with body disposal, the Reinhard camps were achieving what they had been intended for, the wholesale mass extermination of the Jews. (ARC)

Chapter Four

Extermination Camp

Even as the German Army marched across Poland in September 1939, Hitler had already planned the large-scale annexation of the doomed country. When he attained victory at the end of September the Germans acquired territory with a population of over 20 million, of whom 17 million were Poles and 675,000 Germans. Hitler had decided to incorporate large areas of Poland into the *Reich* and agreed on clearing the Poles and Jews out of the incorporated areas and replacing them with German settlers. What followed was a period of more or less unrestrained terror in Poland, particularly in the incorporated territories. The areas that were not incorporated comprised of a population of some 11 million. It included the Polish province of Lublin and parts of the provinces of Warsaw and Krakow. It was initially termed the 'General Government of the Occupied Polish Areas', but in 1940 was renamed the 'General Government'.

By February it had become such a problem of simultaneously attempting to relocate Poles, Jews and the ethnic Germans that it was agreed that the Jews should be forced to live in ghettos. This would not only relieve the burden of the re-settlement programme, but it was a way of temporarily getting rid of the growing Jewish problem. After all, the Nazis hated and feared the Jews and to isolate them in ghettos was deemed immediately practicable for it was believed that Eastern Jews in particular were carriers of diseases and needed to be isolated.

Whilst plans were put into practice creating ghettos, the SS asserted its need to pursue harsh policies in order to deal with the threat of subversion by Polish nationalists and Jewish Bolshevists in the newly incorporated territories. Already by early 1940 the situation in the various detention centres and concentration camps had become untenable due to the new policies of arresting and detaining enemies of the state. News had already circulated through SS channels that government officials were demanding immediate action in the expansion of the concentration camp system through its new conquered territory, Poland. The German authorities quickly pressed forward to establish various camps in Poland where they could be incarcerated and set to work as stonebreakers, and construction workers for buildings and streets. It was envisaged that these Poles would remain as a slave labour force, and it was therefore deemed necessary to erect these so-called 'quarantine camps', in order to subdue the local population. Initially, it had been proposed that the quarantine camps were to hold the prisoners until they were sent to the various other concentration camps in the *Reich*. However, it soon became apparent that this was totally impracticable so it was approved that these camps were to function as a permanent prison for all those that were unfortunate to have been sent there.

Throughout 1940 the SS concentration camp system in Poland began to expand. In April a new camp was created in the Polish Army baracks situated in the town of Oswiecim, which was situated in a remote corner of south-western Poland, in a marshy valley where the Sola River flows into the Vistula about 35 miles west of the ancient city of Krakow. The town was virtually unknown outside Poland and following the occupation of the country Oswiecim was incorporated into the *Reich* together with Upper Silesia and renamed by the German authorities as Auschwitz.

Auschwitz 'labour camp', as it was still known, soon expanded. Yet, in spite of the orchestrated terror and executions at Auschwitz there were features of the concentration camp that were similar to the traditions of Dachau. However, this soon changed as the war entered a new stage, this time against an even greater threat, the Soviet Union.

From the summer of 1941 Auschwitz entered a new era in its ruthless evolution. The guards were not only torturing and killing Polish prisoners but were murdering Russian POWs as well. By the late summer this orgy of death soon escalated when Himmler put forward grander plans of producing a factory-like killing installation that was capable of removing anyone deemed a threat to the *Reich* or unfit for slave labour. Those that were regarded subhuman, for instance like Russian POWs, were certainly on the *Reichsführer's* agenda for liquidation, and it was suggested that it would be practical to use the Russian POWs in a killing experiment. This experiment was undertaken on 3 September 1941 using crystallised prussic acid, which was sold in tins marked under the name of Zyklon B. No longer would the guards have to look into the eyes of their victims as they murdered them. Now they could transport their victims straight into a specially adapted gas chamber and have them killed altogether. The guards found by simple innovation that the new arrivals could quite easily be led into the crematorium not knowing they were going to be killed, simply disinfected by taking a shower. It had proven very easy to get the inmates into the gas chamber by deception rather than using varying degrees of force. By using gas as a method of execution the guards found its implementation less stressful than simply shooting the inmates out of hand in a mass blood bath.

With the success of a gassing facility more prisoners were transported directly to Auschwitz and killed. In late 1941 the camp again evolved with the building of Birkenau, a huge area of land near the main Auschwitz camp.

Now Auschwitz was slowly transformed from a quiet backwater quarantine camp into a dual-function camp.

In the summer of 1942 there was a new change in policy and Auschwitz was given a new role in the implementation of the genocidal solution of what was known as the 'Jewish problem'.

During this period many thousands of Jews, Poles, gypsies and Russian prisoners were transported to Birkenau and either worked to death or sent directly to the makeshift gas chambers.

Over the following year specially constructed crematoria were built at Birkenau aimed purely to murder, and then dispose of the bodies by cremation. The site soon evolved into the largest single mass killing factory in Nazi Europe.

Whilst Auschwitz continued killing thousands of innocent people, across other parts of Poland other extermination camps were also revelling in the orgy of mass murder. In Majdanek for instance some 360,000 Jews were killed over a period of two years. Many of the guards who oversaw the killings in Majdanek, looked upon the gassings as the most humane way to murder. Many of the men that had come to places like Majdnek and Auschwitz considered their posting comfortable, compared to being sent to the Eastern Front to fight the growing might of the Red Army. Here the men lived in relative ease and were rewarded for meting out beatings and various forms of punishments. To be able to freely beat, brutalise and murder the prisoners actually provided some with the opportunity to compensate for feelings of inferiority.

No matter how gruesome the outcome was for these hapless Jews during the last year of the war, the Germans had created the perfect killing factories on an industrial scale. By the summer of 1944 Auschwitz, for instance, had all four crematoria working more or less on a daily basis, killing thousands each day. The ovens continued to work at full capacity and the incineration ditches were being used day and night. The frenetic gassings and burnings carried on for days and weeks regardless of the deteriorating military situation. During July an average of 3,500 each day were arriving at the ramps with more than three-quarters of the new arrivals being sent directly to the crematoria for 'special treatment'. This phenomenal figure certainly demonstrated the guard's efficiency to oversee the 'final solution' with fanatical determination.

A photograph taken at what was known as Auschwitz.I during a visit by Gauleiter Bracht. Rudolf Höss, commandant of Auschwitz, can be seen pictured third from right. (*Auschwitz-Birkenau Museum*)

Jews have been unloaded in an unknown destination. Within about three hours of reaching their destination the old, very young and those too weak to work were often shot or gassed. *(HITM)*

Reichsführer Heinrich Himmler visited Auschwitz-Birkenau in March 1941 and then again in July 1942. Here in this photograph he converses with some of the representatives from the giant industrial chemical conglomerate, I.G. Farben, which was proposing the construction of a synthetic-rubber factory near Auschwitz. It would produce a synthetic rubber called Buna and inmates from Auschwitz would erect the building, and be used as slave labour. The project was very lucrative for the SS. *(Auschwitz-Birkenau Museum)*

A view of the SS retreat at Solahuette. This timber framed building was regarded as an idyllic location for the SS officer's staff of Auschwitz to spend time relaxing and joking. It was a far cry from the horrors less than 30 miles away. (*USHMM*)

Two photographs showing SS troops marching along a road very near to Auschwitz. For many SS guards, their posting to Auschwitz was preferable to having to fight the growing might of the Red Army on the Eastern Front. (*USHMM*)

An SS officer arrives on a visit to Auschwitz. Many SS officers and party officials came to Auschwitz to see for themselves the progress of the expansion programme of the camp, and to meet with the commandant and other members of staff. They even visited occasionally to see firsthand the extermination process. *(Auschwitz-Birkenau Museum)*

Hungarian Jews conversing with some of the German guards on the ramp during selection. *(Auschwitz-Birkenau Museum)*

A photo showing the selection process on the ramp at Auschwitz-Birkenau. Entire families often arrived in Auschwitz, but soon after their arrival they were broken apart. Jews were thrown out of the cattle cars often without their belongings and forced to make two separate lines, men and women/children. SS medical personnel then conducted selections among these lines, sending most victims to the gas chambers where they were usually killed and cremated on the same day. *(Auschwitz-Birkenau Museum/USHMM – Yad Vashem Museum)*

A photograph taken at Auschwitz after the handing over of the new SS hospital. Pictured left to right are Dr Eduard Wirths, Dr Enno Lölling, and Auschwitz Commandant Richard Baer. Standing to their left is adjutant Karl Hoecker, and Rudolf Höss. *(USHMM)*

SS officers relax and converse in groups in the grounds of the SS retreat at Solahutte, outside Auschwitz. From left to right: Josef Kramer, (unidentified), Karl Hocker and Franz Hossler. Just weeks before this photograph was taken, in May 1944, Josef Kramer was put in charge of the gas chambers at the Auschwitz-Birkenau compound. He was to hold that position until December 1944, when he was transferred out as commandant of Belsen. *(USHMM)*

SS officer Karl Hocker salutes in front of an array of wreaths during a military funeral at Auschwitz. The original caption of the photograph reads 'Burying our SS comrades after a terror attack'. *(USHMM)*

SS officers socialise at the SS retreat of Solahuette outside Auschwitz. From left to right they are: Josef Mengele, Richard Baer (commandant of Auschwitz), Karl Hocker (his adjutant) and Walter Schmidetzki (head of Canada – the sorting house where prisoners' property was taken – and later administrative director of Monowitz). *(USHMM)*

At Auschwitz the SS held a number of comradeship meetings in order to try and encourage a sense of solidarity among the men. Although Höss had always found this type of solidarity a charade he nonetheless attended whenever he had time. Here in this photograph SS men sing along to the tune of an accordion at the SS retreat at Solahuette in the summer of 1944. Pictured in the front row are: Karl Hoecker, Otto Moll, Rudolf Höss, Richard Baer, Josef Kramer (standing slightly behind Franz Hössler and partially obscured), Franz Hössler and Josef Mengele. *(USHMM)*

Chapter Five

Woman Concentration Camp Guards

Of the 55,000 guards who served in Nazi concentration camps, about 3,700 were women. In 1942, the first female guards arrived at Auschwitz and Majdanek from Ravensbrück. The year after, the Germans began conscripting women because of a guard shortage. Most women who were recruited to become overseers were middle to low class, had no work experience, and their professional background varied. As a group, the women guards were not highly regarded by their inmates, who were often educationally and culturally their superiors. Volunteers were mostly German women who were recruited by ads in newspapers asking women to show their love for the *Reich* by joining the *SS-Gefolge* (an SS cousin organisation for women). A few entered the service this way, attracted by the promise of light physical work and good wages. But countless young women were recruited under stronger incentives from SS officials. They were told to choose between continuing their menial position indefinitely or joining the SS. The position of a women guard paid well, and in 1944, an unmarried women guard in her mid-twenties could make about 100 Reichmarks more than she could as a textile worker. By 1943, the *Reich* Labour Ministry was empowered to conscript women between seventeen and forty-five years of age for labour service, and by the end of that same year, most of the women reporting for concentration camp training were conscripts.

Ravensbrück served as the main training ground for some 3,700 female guards after 1938. Trainees spent anywhere from a week to six months at the camp, at first being given regulated instruction from the head overseer. The trainees were taught the standard regulations applicable to all concentration camps, 'how to detect sabotage and work slowdowns, how to prevent escapes, and how to punish prisoners within the parameters of camp regulations'. It was emphasised that female guards were to have no relationship of a personal nature at all with any of the prisoners. The guards were notoriously cruel. The nicknames given to some of the guards, such as the 'Beast of Auschwitz' and the 'Bitch of Buchenwald', are clear evidence of the brutality that reigned in the camps.

The code of conduct for these female guards was based solely upon the SS demand for absolute obedience to all orders from SS superior officers, and upon their insistence that each prisoner be treated with fanatical hatred as an enemy of the state.

Helga Hegal was one such recruit that became officially known as a female SS concentration camp guard or *SS-Gefolge*. During the early part of the war she worked in a little family grocery shop in Düsseldorf with her parents and appeared a very outwardly friendly and thoughtful young girl. However, one day in the spring of 1942, when she was passing the city hall she noticed two young SS soldiers handing out leaflets appealing for female recruits to join the *SS-Gefolge*. Within a few days and without telling her father, Helga decided to go along to a nearby *Waffen-SS* recruiting office. Almost immediately Helga accepted her new role and a few weeks later received her papers to train as an *SS-Gefolge*. The thought of joining as a guard in a concentration camp appealed immensely to Helga and was far removed from her boring existence selling fruit and vegetables. She told her father that she had been given a job with in an administration department of the SS in Ravensbrück.

In August 1942 Helga finally left Düsseldorf to begin her new life within the realms of the SS. At the city hall Helga and her comrades were split into small groups, given their individual destinations, and then transported to various stations where they boarded trains. Helga and her group arrived late in the evening and were directed by military police to the main camp, where they reported to the central administration building and were allocated 'provisional' bunks in the SS barracks.

The following day Helga and the rest of the new recruits were in training, and almost immediately they were told by their superior officers to hate the inmates, especially the Jewish prisoners. She was told to regard all prisoners as subhuman adversaries of the state, and those who offered the slightest resistance were marked for immediate destruction. Though not violently anti-Semitic at the time, she was told to consider the Jews the most dangerous of all the enemies of National Socialism. To supplement the indoctrination process she learnt the art of corporal punishment. This usually consisted of twenty-five lashes with a whip, carried out in the presence of the assembled female and male guards, all the prisoners and the camp commandant. It was normally the camp commandant who rotated the responsibility for these whippings. Constantly the guards were ordered to treat the prisoners harshly and impersonally, and to remain disciplined and avoid embarrassing inquiries. The camp commanders told them to be pitiless and cruelly insensitive to human suffering, and not to show qualities such as mercy and charity.

Many young German women appeared to be attracted by their new role, in spite of the fact that many of them did not know what was actually in store for them. But once they were in training the prestige of the uniform, elitism, toughness, and comradeship soon outweighed any morale scruples. Some almost enjoyed meting out harsh and often brutal punishments for the slightest infractions of camp rules.

New recruits spent three weeks every month in training, followed by one week of guard duty within the concentration camp. At the end of training, the recruits were selected and sent out to the various concentration camps. As soon as they arrived the guards were allotted their barracks, given their uniforms and then detailed the next day on a variety of duties they would have to perform. Gertrude Mitte was a young twenty-three-year-old single machinist from Münster who had been recruited to help the SS guards at Belzec concentration camp. SS *Hauptsturmführer* Christian Wirth was the commandant of the camp and nicknamed by the SS guards as 'savage Christian', Wirth was a sadist. He was once observed whipping a Jewish woman and chasing her into the gas chamber, and he personally murdered Jews with his own hands. Red faced and sweating he was regularly seen screaming obscenities while encouraging his men to commit bestial acts. Small though it was, Belzec was not simply a camp. Wirth knew that the key to the smooth functioning of his death factory was concealing the true purpose of the place from new arrivals for long as possible. So within the camp he enclosed the gas chambers in a special area known as Camp 2, which was hidden behind trees and wire fences woven through with branches. This area was connected to the rest of the camp only by 'the tube', a passageway through the wire. Camp 1 – the rest of Belzec – consisted of the arrival area next to the railway, various barracks where new arrivals undressed and where their belongings could be stored before being transported out. Gertrude's first duty in Belzec was to assist the Ukrainian guards and to carry out basic supervisionary duties in the camp. Famed for their brutality, many of these Ukrainians having previously fought in the Red Army had been trained by the Germans, and were allowed this opportunity to escape the terrible conditions of the POW camps. Gertrude found the Ukrainians unpleasant and coarse, on account of them taking a general liking to the female overseers.

Whilst Gertrude was assigned to the disinfection room other female overseers ensured the calm arrival of the Jews from the cattle cars. Using an oxide whip and wearing a side cap distinctly displaying the infamous *Totenkopf* death-head badge, they assisted both German and Ukrainian guards supervising the new arrivals. Each member of the camp was trained to dupe all new arrivals into believing they had stopped briefly at a disinfecting stop where they would be treated as a precaution against disease, and were then to be hurried through the camp to their deaths as quickly as possible. Although Gertrude initially found the whole spectacle uncomfortable, once she had been working at the camp for a number of weeks her work had become more or less routine.

Yet, Gertrude was one of a number of women guards that worked and lived in the concentration camps without ever wanting to conduct extreme acts of brutality and blood lust. But despite this more restrained approach towards the inmates, there were many female guards who entered the realms of the concentration camp system determined to prove that they could be as evil or more evil than their male counterparts.

Dorothea Binz, an attractive, slim looking women, was one new recruit whom Gertrude met one cold morning in late 1942. Whilst off duty she used to play chess and joke and giggle with her other female comrades. But on duty Binz was one of the most depraved and cruel women guards in the concentration camp. At only twenty-five years old she had become the chief wardress of the women's cell block building. Even by SS standards, Binz's behaviour was atrocious. Gertrude would sometimes have to watch as Binz beat, kicked, slapped and whipped prisoners ruthlessly. She seemed to take great pride in the fact that her mere presence caused the inmates to tremble with fear. She gleefully followed the policy of controlled and disciplined terror laid down by Eicke in the early days of SS guard training. In effect, this barbarous woman could conduct her cruel beatings with a nonchalant and cavalier attitude.

It is difficult to say if Gertrude or her comrades ever learned anything from Binz in the way of perversity and cruelty, but Binz and a number of other women guards close to her are remembered by survivors for their 'special treatments'. In both cases, many of the women seemed to enjoy sex coupled with bizarre sadistic behaviour in torturing the inmates. Binz, who formerly had been a maid, walked about the compound with a whip and a dog, often accompanied by her boyfriend, SS Schtuz-haftlagerführer Edmund Brauning. In fact, the real attention was generally focussed on the two lovers as they stood arm-in-arm enjoying the spectacle of public floggings. After the pain had been inflicted, the two would then kiss and cuddle.

Another female guard who was synonymous with inflicting various forms of brutality on the inmates was a young woman called Irma Grese. In 1943, at only twenty years old she was transferred from Ravensbrück to Auschwitz, where she became Oberaufseherin (senior matron), controlling thirty-one barracks housing some 30,000 women. Although she had mistreated prisoners at Ravensbrück, Auschwitz afforded her much greater opportunities for doing evil. Tidy, immaculately groomed, she walked about the camp with her black boots, whip and smart looking SS uniform looking for victims she could torture or kill. Grese was obsessive about tidiness and good order, which was, of course, very much a German cultural trait.

It did not take long before she became known as 'the Auschwitz Angel of Death'. As she stood before the prisoners, immaculately dressed in her uniform, Irma could smile and be outwardly nice, but at the same time could be very cruel. Witnesses saw her shoot a mother and child in the camp when they caused her trouble, whilst to others she could offer kind words. Often Irma accompanied Dr Josef Mengele on inspection tours of the women's quarters and helped him make gas chamber selections there. Whenever Mengele saw a young and pretty prisoner, Irma would choose this girl for a trip to the bathhouse.

Irma had many other lovers, including SS officers and prisoners of both genders. She frequently enjoyed homosexual relations with these prisoners and then sent them straight to their deaths. One particular female who took her eye was a young block leader called Rachelle, and they soon became lesbian lovers. One night after an argument Irma sent Rachelle back to her barracks and then added her name to the next day's 'selection' list.

On another occasion, Irma picked for her lover a tall, attractive prisoner from Soviet Georgia. The muscular Georgian had been assigned to a male work detail in the women's camp. Calling him into her office, Irma made it clear what she wanted. But he turned her down. Enraged, Irma summoned his girlfriend, a pretty Polish teenager, and made him watch while she stripped and lashed the terrified youngster. Then she had the Georgian shot and the girl sent to the Auschwitz brothel, from where she was eventually sent to her death in Mengele's laboratory.

When not engaged in sex and sadism, Irma spent hours grooming herself in front of the mirror. Strange though it may seem before Irma arrived at Auschwitz she showed no signs of becoming a sadist. By all accounts she lived a modest life in a loving family environment. It was the circumstances of Auschwitz that made Irma become a fearful and hateful person among the prisoners.

Irma was, in many respects, the archetypal guard in Auschwitz. Perfectly turned out on every occasion, she had utter contempt for the inmates. Yet the idea of intimate relationships with prisoners actually appealed to her, despite her hatred for them. It was far from the typical Nazi ideal, where it was instilled in every guard and SS officer that those imprisoned in the camp represented a danger to the physical well-being of the *Reich*, sexual relationships between members of the SS and camp inmates were expressly forbidden. Such acts constituted as a 'race crime' for the Germans. Killing Jewish women was, it seems, a sacred ideological duty of the SS, but having sex with them was a crime. But many of the male and female guards were having sexual relations, however cruel or bestial the act was for them.

Sexual relations between female guards and SS men were tolerated in the concentration camps and became commonplace in the daily life. Luise Danz was a woman guard who regularly indulged herself in various forms of sexual acts with guards and prisoners. She had been transferred into Birkenau from Plaszow labour camp, and began to work jointly with Grese in the actual administration of BII/c. Fanatically devoted to their mission to eliminate those determined as subhuman, Danz met Grese at 7.00am, usually every day of the week. Irma always led the way accompanied by Danz into the camp, whilst the other female guards followed closely behind. Almost as soon as she passed through the gate Grese and her accomplices spread both physical and physiological terror independently throughout the camp.

Irma Grese's terroristic abuse of the prisoners was occasionally restrained by her male superiors, Auschwitz Commandant Rudolf Höss, acting on orders from *SS-Reichsführer* Heinrich Himmler, made Grese administer the last two of twenty-five strikes with a rubber truncheon to a female guard who had been accused of being too lenient on prisoners. The punished guard was then dragged away and the following day was forced to make selections with Grese for slave labour. Hatred for the inmates was paramount, and Grese watched closely as the guard made her selections, ensuring that she showed no pity for them whatsoever.

One wardress that was never accused of being too lenient on the prisoners was Juana Bormann. At only twenty-five years old she was proud to be wearing her SS uniform and spreading fear among the camp. Juana returned to Ravensbrück *en route* to her new duty station in Poland. Juana had arrived as a trainee at Ravensbrück at approximately the same time that a new commandant was appointed, and this marked a distinct turning point in the camp's history. Fritz Suhren assumed command in July 1942, and conditions soon deteriorated, human experimentation began, and new methods of oppressing inmates were further implemented. Juana Bormann's primary assignments at Ravensbrück had been to oversee work details. Now, in March 1943, Juana headed east provided with orders to report to Auschwitz. Here in southern Poland she would be able to carry out her mission – to oppress and eliminate undesirables of the *Reich*.

Upon her arrival she soon waged an unquenchable thirst of brutality against the inmates. Although she had committed atrocities at Ravensbrück, it was at Auschwitz-Birkenau-Monowitz complex where she truly earned her notorious reputation. Upon completion of her guard training, she was given the rank of a matron, which was regarded as the hardest, the toughest of all the woman guards.

In addition to supervising labour and punishment details, Juana was assigned to other routine duties within the Auschwitz facility. She, and a fellow matron called Elisabeth Volkenrath, was also assigned to different jobs such as a telephone operator, and Juana was made the commander of a gardening squad.

Life for Juana at Auschwitz was good and what made existence there even more comfortable for her and her fellow comrades was the fact that they were able to steal from the dead. Corruption at Auschwitz, and indeed many of the other camps, were largely integrated into the female administrative system. The temptations for the SS and the female guards were irresistible and as a result, stealing was commonplace. Juana and her fellow comrade Ulrika Ramus soon learnt how easy it was to steal.

Surprisingly, the supervision of the SS members and female guards was actually loose. As a result there were so many opportunities to steal that it was hard to imagine that any of the SS members and female guards were free from involvement in this crime. From a female guard who wanted a new radio to the SS officer who dealt in stolen jewellery, corruption at the camps was on a huge scale.

One of the most famous examples of corruption included Ilse Koch, known as 'the Bitch of Buchenwald', who was the chief female guard at the Buchenwald camp, and married to the camp commandant, Karl Koch. Both embezzled large sums of money and afforded themselves free access to the inmates' belongings; there is also evidence that the Kochs had witnesses to their misdeeds murdered.

When Juana was transferred to Bergen-Belsen in late 1944 she had packed her suitcase containing not only her belongings, but stolen jewellery and money in various currencies. Journeying to Bergen-Belsen she hoped the fruits of a new camp would yield further temptations, but when she arrived there was utter confusion. Here she noticed that the camp was a gigantic typhus graveyard that merely blended into the tranquil countryside.

Bergen-Belsen, in fact, was never a concentration camp or a death camp – at least technically. The facility had been originally created as a model repatriation transit centre for the so-called privileged Jews. By the end of 1944, Bergen-Belsen was designated a sick camp, but with the appointment of *SS-Hauptsturmführer* Josef Kramer to command the camp, unrestrained brutality and terror became the order of the day. To add to this, the masses of prisoners from the eastern death camps, particularly those from Auschwitz complex, overwhelmed Bergen-Belsen and it quickly evolved into an open stockade with insufficient housing and tremendous overcrowding. Bergen-Belsen had doubled its size, and food became virtually non-existent.

As soon as Juana arrived she was assigned immediately to issuing accurate roll call duties.

Weeks later her immediate superior Irma Grese arrived. The Belsen commandant, Kramer, had already reassigned Irma, but she asked him if she could stay. Kramer, a man who was reputed to be one of her many lovers, authorised Grese to have her permanent assignment at Belsen. To her female colleagues it seemed that SS Matron Grese wanted to remain at the typhus-ridden hell-hole just for the love of her SS boyfriend. Yet, Juana soon found out that Irma was in fact secretly having an affair with an SS guard who she referred always as '*her Hatchi*'. Hatchi was in fact *SS-Oberscharführer* Franz Hatzinger. Both Hatzinger and Grese had met each other whilst they were stationed at Auschwitz. He was a married man and fourteen years older than Grese, but it was clear to Juana that they were very close and regularly sloped off secretly to have sex.

Another female guard at Belsen who wanted to stay for the love of another SS guard was none other than Elisabeth Volkenrath. Her opportunity to stay at Bergen-Belsen, like Grese, would ultimately put her own life in jeopardy as the allies rapidly approached from the west. But both women had resigned themselves to stay, whatever the outcome. In spite of the deteriorating military situation it still did not deter the women from continuing the same sort of terror and cruelty that they had become notorious for at Birkenau. Although all the guards at Belsen were fully aware that the prisoners were dying all around them and typhus was rife throughout the camp, Grese and Volkenrath would nonetheless order frail, emaciated prisoners to undergo strenuous exercises, including holding heavy rocks over their heads for extended periods of time.

Even as the war neared its end in April 1945, both the female and male guards continued upholding their mission to murder and be cruel. Despite the impending collapse of the Third *Reich*, the majority of the women guards did not attempt to prepare themselves for the inevitable end. Even as the audible sounds of enemy gunfire became louder with each passing day, most of the women, unlike their male counterparts, never tried to gain favour with the inmates by treating them better, even when it was clear to them that Germany would lose the war. With the advance of British forces into the area, the female guards remained at their post, as well as the commandant, Josef Kramer.

The advance units of the British Second Army that liberated Bergen-Belsen on 15 April were not prepared for what they encountered when they arrived at the gates of the camp. British soldiers were horrified by what they saw, smelled and heard in the Lüneburg forest. Yet, even beyond this grotesque sight, the liberation of the camp witnessed some strange moments. As the troops approached the main gates, SS personnel, as if preparing for a formal reception, were drawn up in their field grey uniforms. The SS guards appeared cheerful. Josef Kramer for instance seemed friendly, and cheerful. However, behind them were 10,000 unburied dead in addition to the mass graves already containing 40,000 more corpses. At that time as many as 500 a day were perishing from the long-term effects of starvation as well as the resultant diseases. After many of the SS personnel were taken into custody, Kramer spoke of the starving masses as if they were animals. He appeared more concerned that the British would use their loudspeakers, fearing it might cause the inmates to stampede. Then as the British moved further into the camp, the sound of periodic gunfire could be heard. SS guards were firing on inmates surging toward the kitchen in hope of finding something to eat. Irma Grese attacked a British General as he was attempting to enter some huts, but she was immediately restrained.

When the British came upon the women's compound, the troops were confronted by a formation of well-fed overweight female guards who were said to be casually standing around chatting and smoking cigarettes. All the women wore white brassards on their lower left tunic sleeves with a black cloth strip bearing the silver threaded *SS-Aufseherin* stamp. One soldier recalled that many of the women had contorted, ugly facial expressions and all wore either hobnailed jack boots or military issue dress shoes with black socks.

Once the SS women were arrested, they joined the men on burial details. All of them had the gruesome task of dragging corpses to the pits. The soldiers noticed that the majority of the women had a different reaction to this horrific work than the men did. While some of the men ran away and committed suicide, none of the women did. For them, they had undertaken their evil acts of brutality and for the best part, were proud of carrying it out.

A photograph showing members of the SS female auxiliaries (*Helferinnen*) and SS officer Karl Hocker, who can be seen standing next to the women eating bowls of blueberries. This photograph was taken at an SS retreat called Solahuette not far from Auschwitz. This timber framed building was regarded as an idyllic location for the SS officer's staff of Auschwitz to spend time relaxing and joking. It was a far cry from the horrors less than 30 miles away. (*USHMM*)

A time for joking and singing. Here members of the SS female auxiliaries (*Helferinen*) and some SS guards smile in front of the camera to the sound of an accordion. SS officer Karl Hocker can be seen in the middle smiling with these playful auxiliaries. (*USHMM*)

A photograph of three members of the SS female auxiliary unit employed at Auschwitz. In total there were some 55,000 guards who served in Nazi concentration camps; of these about 3,700 were women. In 1942, the first female guards arrived at Auschwitz and Majdanek from Ravensbrück. The year after, the Nazis began conscripting women because of a guard shortage. (*USHMM*)

Two photographs taken in sequence showing SS officers, including Karl Hocker and SS female auxiliary staff, taking time away from the killing ground of Auschwitz on a day trip to the mountains in southern Poland. (*USHMM*)

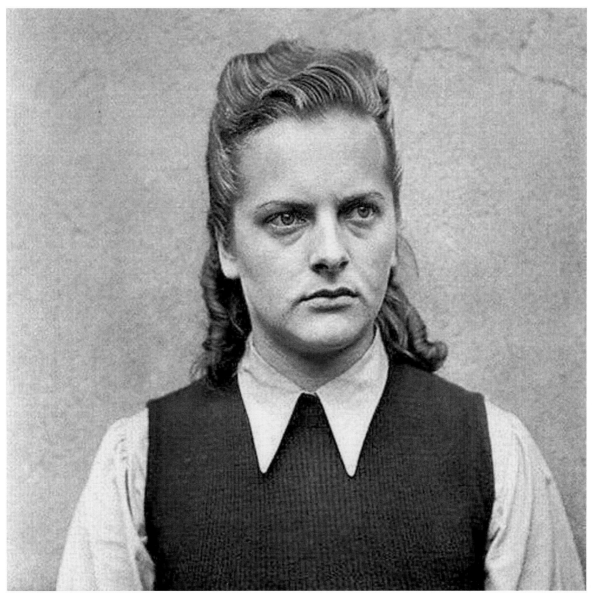

One woman who was synonymous for inflicting various forms of brutality on concentration camp inmates was called Irma Grese. In 1943, at only twenty years old she was transferred from Ravensbrück to Auschwitz, where she became *Oberaufseherin* or senior matron, controlling thirty-one barracks housing some 30,000 women. It did not take long before she became known as 'the Auschwitz Angel of Death'. As she stood before the prisoners, immaculately dressed in her uniform, Irma could smile and be outwardly nice, but at the same time could be very cruel. *(IWM)*

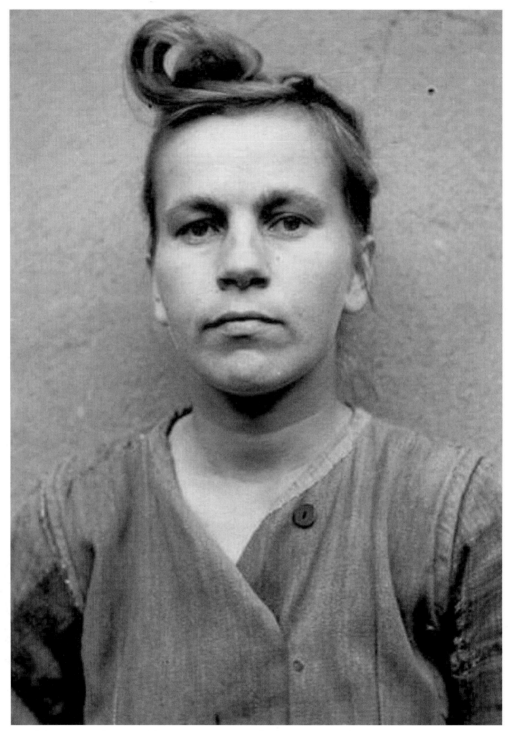

A mugshot of the captured matron Elisabeth Volkenrath. She was sent to Auschwitz where she supervised labour and punishment details. She was also assigned other routine duties within the Auschwitz facility including telephone operator. Later in the war Volkenrath was transferred to Bergen-Belsen. Although she and the guards were fully aware that the prisoners were dying all around them and typhus was rife throughout the camp, Volkenrath together with Grese would order frail, emaciated prisoners to undergo strenuous exercises, including making inmates hold heavy rocks over their heads for extended periods of time. She was captured at Belsen in 1945. (*IWM*)

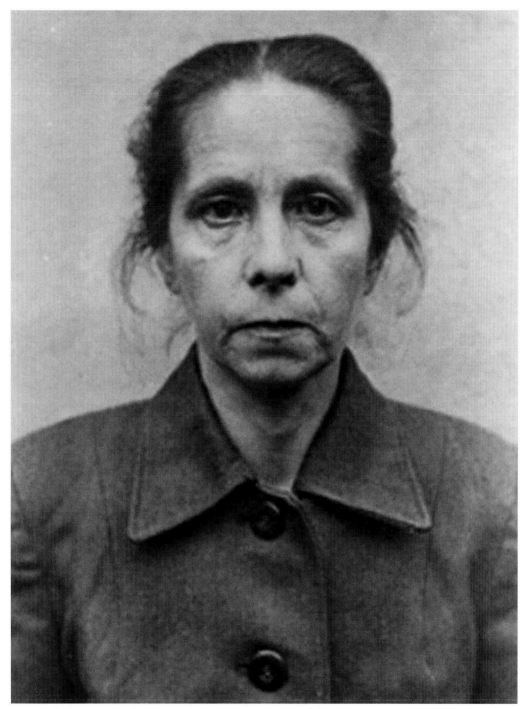

Another mug shot, this time of Juana Bormann just before her trial. As a concentration camp guard she was one wardress that was never accused of being too lenient on the prisoners. At only twenty-five years old she was proud to be wearing her SS uniform and spreading fear among the camp. Following a stint at Ravensbrück she was transferred to Auschwitz where she soon waged an unquenchable thirst of brutality against the inmates. It was at the Auschwitz-Birkenau-Monowitz complex where she truly earned her notorious reputation. Upon completion of her guard training, she was given the rank of a matron, which was regarded the hardest and toughest of all the woman guards. (IWM)

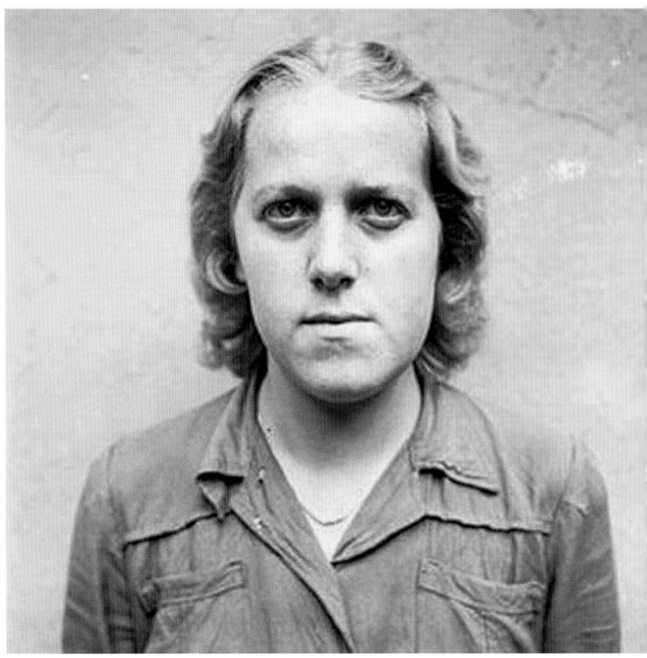

A photograph of the notorious Herta Bothe awaiting trial in August 1945. In September 1942 she was conscripted to Ravensbrück concentration camp. The former nurse underwent four weeks of intensive training. Following her training she was sent to the Stutthof camp near Danzig where she earned the name as the 'sadist of Stutthof' due to the terrible beatings and tortures she inflicted on the prisoners. Later in the war she was transferred to Auschwitz where she helped in the death march to Belsen. Once at Belsen, Bothe was put in charge of sixty prisoners that were conscripted into a wood cutting brigade. It was here in Belsen that this ruthless overseer was captured. After being captured she was given the gruesome task of helping bury the dead. She survived the hangman's noose and received only a short prison sentence. (IWM)

Maria Mandel

Taken following her arrest is Maria Mandel. She became a top ranking official at Auschwitz where she was believed to have been responsible for the deaths of over 500,000 female prisoners. Her humble beginnings before she became one of the most infamous women concentration murderers began in 1942 when she was given the rank of *SS-Oberaufseherin* at Ravensbrück. She was assigned to regularly beat and flog the prisoners until she was sent to Auschwitz-Birkenau. It was here she succeeded Johanna Langefeld as an *SS-Lagerführerin*. She was the highest ranking female guard at Auschwitz and directly under the commandant Rudolf Höss, who was the only man Mandel reported to. Mandel controlled the female Auschwitz camps and female subcamps. For the next two years she participated extensively in selections for death and was known to have enjoyed choosing children for the gas chambers. It did not take long before she became known as the 'beast'. By the end of 1944 she was assigned to Mühldorf subcamp of Dachau. She was captured by the US Army in May 1945 after fleeing into the Austrian mountains. She was later tried in Krakow for war crimes and hanged on 24 January 1948 at the age of thirty-six. (*US Army*)

A posed photo showing *SS-Hauptsturmführer* Josef Kramer after his arrest at Bergen-Belsen. With the advance of British forces into the area, the female guards remained at their post, including the commandant, Josef Kramer. Bergen-Belsen had been designated as a sick camp at the end of 1944, but with the appointment of Kramer to command the camp, unrestrained brutality and terror became the order of the day. Kramer was dubbed 'The Beast of Belsen' and worked very closely with the women guards. Before his assignment to Belsen he was at Auschwitz where he had been put in charge of the gas chambers. In December 1944 this brutal man was appointed commandant of Belsen but within five months he was captured by the British. On 13 December 1945 he was hanged. *(IWM, BU3749)*

Two photographs showing the disposal of bodies. Once the SS women were arrested, they joined the men on burial details. All of them had the gruesome task of dragging corpses to the pits. While some of the men ran away and committed suicide, none of the women attempted to avoid it. For them, they had undertaken their evil acts of brutality and for the best part, were proud of carrying them out. *(IWM)*

Another photograph showing the disposal of bodies. *(IWM)*

Survivors and American soldiers watch as former SS guards are forced to crouch in front of their captors. (*USHMM*)

Survivors attack a former guard at Bergen-Belsen. Such scenes were often a common sight and many SS guards were murdered in revenge killings. *(IWM)*

SS guards clearly displaying the infamous *Totenkopf* insignia were captured and detained by their British captors. One British soldier can be seen going through an SS guard's personal belongs, including his identity card. (*IWM*)

A photograph taken following the capture of women guards at Bergen-Belsen in April 1945. When the British came upon the women's compound at Bergen-Belsen, the troops were confronted by a formation of well-fed overweight female guards who were said to be casually standing around chatting and smoking cigarettes. All the women wore white brassards on their lower left tunic sleeves with a black cloth strip bearing the silver threaded *SS-Aufseherin* stamp. One soldier recalled that many of the women had contorted; ugly facial expressions and all wore either hobnailed jack boots or military issue dress shoes with black socks. *(IWM)*

Trial and retribution for their dreadful deeds. Here Ilse Koch leaves the courtroom with her co-defendants during her trial. Koch began her humble beginnings in the concentration camps as a secretary at Sachsenhausen. She came to Buchenwald when her husband, Otto Koch, was made commandant. Koch was later arrested by the SS for private enrichment and embezzlement and was not released until 1944 for lack of evidence, but her husband was executed in Buchenwald in April 1945. Koch and thirty others were accused of war crimes in front of an American military court. She was charged, however, for aiding and abetting in murders on inmates and was given life imprisonment. However, three years later she was acquitted and in 1952 committed suicide. (*USHMM*)

Appendix

List of Camps

Camp	Function	Location	Est.	Evacuated	Liberated	Estimated Murdered
Auschwitz	Concentration/Extermination	Oswiecim, Poland (near Krakow)	26 May 1940	18 Jan 1945	27 Jan 27 1945 by Soviets	1,100,000
Belzec	Extermination	Belzec, Poland	17 March 1942		Liquidated by Nazis December 1942	600,000
Bergen-Belsen	Detention; Concentration (After 3/44)	near Hanover, Germany	April 1943		15 April 1945 by British	35,000
Buchenwald	Concentration	Buchenwald, Germany (near Weimar)	16 July 1937	6 April 1945	11 April 1945 Self-Liberated; 11 April 1945 by Americans	
Chelmno	Extermination	Chelmno, Poland	7 Dec 1941; 23 June 1944		Closed March 1943 (but reopened); Liquidated by Nazis July 1944	320,000
Dachau	Concentration	Dachau, Germany (near Munich)	22 March 1933	26 April 1945	29 April 1945 by Americans	32,000
Dora/Mittelbau	Subcamp of Buchenwald; Concentration (After 10/44)	near Nordhausen, Germany	27 Aug 1943	1 April 1945	9 April 1945 by Americans	
Drancy	Assembly/Detention	Drancy, France (suburb of Paris)	August 1941		17 Aug 1944 by Allied Forces	
Flossenbürg	Concentration	Flossenbürg, Germany (near Nuremberg)	3 May 1938	20 April 1945	23 April 1945 by Americans	
Gross-Rosen	Subcamp of Sachsenhausen; Concentration (After 5/41)	near Wroclaw, Poland	August 1940	13 Feb 1945	8 May 1945 by Soviets	40,000
Janowska	Concentration/Extermination	L'viv, Ukraine	Sept 1941		Liquidated by Nazis November 1943	
Kaiserwald/Riga	Concentration (After 3/43)	Meza-Park, Latvia (near Riga)	1942	July 1944		
Koldichevo	Concentration	Baranovichi, Belarus	Summer 1942			22,000
Majdanek	Concentration/Extermination	Lublin, Poland	16 Feb 1943	July 1944	22 July 1944 by Soviets	360,000
Mauthausen	Concentration	Mauthausen, Austria (near Linz)	8 Aug 1938		5 May 1945 by Americans	120,000
Natzweiler/Struthof	Concentration	Natzweiler, France (near Strasbourg)	1 May 1941	Sept 1944		12,000
Neuengamme	Subcamp of Sachsenhausen; Concentration (After 6/40)	Hamburg, Germany	13 Dec 1938	29 April 1945	May 1945 by British	56,000
Plaszow	Concentration (After 1/44)	Krakow, Poland	Oct. 1942	Summer 1944	15 Jan 1945 by Soviets	8,000
Ravensbrück	Concentration	near Berlin, Germany	15 May 1939	23 April 1945	30 April 1945 by Soviets	
Sachsenhausen	Concentration	Berlin, Germany	July 1936	March 1945	27 April 1945 by Soviets	
Sered	Concentration	Sered, Slovakia (near Bratislava)	1941/42		1 April 1945 by Soviets	
Sobibor	Extermination	Sobibor, Poland (near Lublin)	March 1942	Revolt on 14 October 1943; Liquidated by Nazis October 1943	Summer 1944 by Soviets	250,000
Stutthof	Concentration (After 1/42)	near Danzig, Poland	Sept. 2, 1939	25 Jan 1945	9 May 1945 by Soviets	65,000
Theresienstadt	Concentration	Terezin, Czech Republic (near Prague)	24 Nov 1941	Handed over to Red Cross 3 May 1945	8 May 1945 by Soviets	33,000
Treblinka	Extermination	Treblinka, Poland (near Warsaw)	July 23, 1942	Revolt on 2 April 1943; Liquidated by the SS April 1943		800,000
Vaivara	Concentration/Transit	Estonia	Sept 1943		Closed 28 June 1944	
Westerbork	Transit	Westerbork, Netherlands	Oct. 1939		12 April 1945 camp handed over to Kurt Schlesinger	

Glossary and Abbreviations

Einsatzgruppen	Mobile killing units of the SS, *Sipo-SD*.
Gau	One of forty-two administrative districts into which the Nazi Germany was divided.
Gauleiter	Nazi Party boss in a gau.
General Government	Occupied part of eastern Poland not annexed to Germany.
Gestapo	*Geheime Staatspolizei*, state secret police.
Kapo	Privileged prisoner who served as a barracks supervisor/warder or lead work detail in a Nazi concentration camp/labour camp or death camp.
Reichsführer-SS	*Reich* Chief of the SS and German Police.
RSHA	*Reichssicherheitshauptamt*, *Reich* Main Security Office, formed in late 1939, uniting Gestapo, criminal police, SIPO and SD.
Sipo	*Sicherheitspolizei*, security police of the Nazi Party.
SD	*Sicherheitsdienst*, security service of the Nazi Party.
Sonderkommando	Special unit of SS.
SS *Schutzstaffel,*	Guard Detachment created in 1925 as elite Nazi Party bodyguard that evolved in a security and intelligence service with a military arm.
Totenkopf	*Totenkopfverbände*, 'Death's Head', unit of SS deployed to guard concentration camps.
Waffen-SS	Weapon SS, military arm of the SS from 1939 onwards.
Wehrmacht	German armed forces but excluding the *Waffen-SS*.
WVHA	*Wirtschaffts und Verwaltungshauptamt*, SS Economic and Administrative Head Office, responsible for SS economic enterprises and concentration camps from 1942 under the command of Oswald Pohl.

Rank Equivalents

German Army	*Waffen-SS*	British Army
Gemeiner, Landser	*Schütze*	Private
	Oberschütze	
Grenadier	*Sturmmann*	Lance Corporal
Obergrenadier		

German Army	Waffen-SS	British Army
Gefreiter	Rottenführer	Corporal
Obergefreiter	Unterscharführer	
Stabsgefreiter		
Unteroffizier	Scharführer	Sergeant
Unterfeldwebel	Oberscharführer	Colour Sergeant
Feldwebel		
Oberfeldwebel	Hauptscharführer	Sergeant Major
Stabsfeldwebel	Hauptbereitschaftsleiter	
	Sturmscharführer	Warrant Officer
Leutnant	Untersturmführer	Second Lieutenant
Oberleutnant	Obersturmführer	First Lieutenant
Hauptmann	Hauptsturmführer	Captain
Major	Sturmbannführer	Major
Oberstleutnant	Obersturmbannführer	Lieutenant Colonel
Oberst	Standartenführer	Colonel
	Oberführer	Brigadier General
Generalmajor	Brigadeführer	Major General
Generalleutnant	Gruppenführer	Lieutenant General
General	Obergruppenführer	General
Generaloberst	Oberstgruppenführer	
Generalfeldmarschall	Reichsführer-SS	